Francis Frith's

# Essex

## A Second Selection

RUSSELL THOMPSON was born in Chelmsford in 1965, and educated at the town's Grammar School. He now works in adult education as a creative writing tutor. At other times, he is in demand as a performance-poet, and has recently completed a show at the Edinburgh Festival. Essex, however, is his first love. He is especially keen on Braintree and Panfield.

*Photographic Memories*

# Francis Frith's
# Essex
## A Second Selection

Russell Thompson

First published in the United Kingdom in 2002 by
Frith Book Company Ltd

Hardback Edition 2002
ISBN 1-85937-456-5

Paperback Edition 2004
ISBN 1-85937-889-7



British Library Cataloguing in Publication Data

Francis Frith's Essex - A Second Selection
Russell Thompson

Frith Book Company Ltd
Frith's Barn, Teffont,
Salisbury, Wiltshire SP3 5QP
Tel: +44 (0) 1722 716 376
Email: info@francisfrith.co.uk
www.francisfrith.co.uk

Printed and bound in Great Britain

Front Cover: Waltham Abbey, Market Square 1921 70158

*The colour-tinting is for illustrative purposes only, and is not intended to be historically accurate*

AS WITH ANY HISTORICAL DATABASE THE FRITH ARCHIVE IS CONSTANTLY BEING CORRECTED AND IMPROVED AND THE PUBLISHERS WOULD WELCOME INFORMATION ON OMISSIONS OR INACCURACIES

# Contents

# Francis Frith: *Victorian Pioneer*

**Francis Frith**, Victorian founder of the world-famous photographic archive, was a complex and multi-talented man. A devout Quaker and a highly successful Victorian businessman, he was both philosophical by nature and pioneering in outlook.

By 1855 Francis Frith had already established a wholesale grocery business in Liverpool, and sold it for the astonishing sum of £200,000, which is the equivalent today of over £15,000,000. Now a very rich man, he was able to indulge his passion for travel. As a child he had pored over travel books written by early explorers, and his fancy and imagination had been stirred by family holidays to the sublime mountain regions of Wales and Scotland. 'What lands of spirit-stirring and enriching scenes and places!' he had written. He was to return to these scenes of grandeur in later years to 'recapture the thousands of vivid and tender memories', but with a different purpose. Now in his thirties, and captivated by the new science of photography, Frith set out on a series of pioneering journeys to the Nile regions that occupied him from 1856 until 1860.

### Intrigue and Adventure

He took with him on his travels a specially-designed wicker carriage that acted as both dark-room and sleeping chamber. These far-flung journeys were packed with intrigue and adventure. In his life story, written when he was sixty-three, Frith tells of being held captive by bandits, and of fighting 'an awful midnight battle to the very point of surrender with a deadly pack of hungry, wild dogs'. Sporting flowing Arab costume, Frith arrived at Akaba by camel sixty years before Lawrence, where he encountered 'desert princes and rival sheikhs, blazing with jewel-hilted swords'.

During these extraordinary adventures he was assiduously exploring the desert regions bordering the Nile and patiently recording the antiquities and peoples with his camera. He was the first photographer to venture beyond the sixth cataract. Africa was still the mysterious 'Dark Continent', and Stanley and Livingstone's historic meeting was a decade into the future. The conditions for picture taking confound belief. He laboured for hours in his wicker dark-room in the sweltering heat of the desert, while the volatile chemicals fizzed dangerously in their trays. Often he was forced to work in remote tombs and caves where conditions were cooler. Back in London he exhibited his photographs and was 'rapturously cheered' by members of the Royal Society. His reputation as a photographer was made overnight. An eminent modern historian has likened their impact on the population of the time to that on our own generation of the first photographs taken on the surface of the moon.

## Venture of a Life-Time

Characteristically, Frith quickly spotted the opportunity to create a new business as a specialist publisher of photographs. He lived in an era of immense and sometimes violent change. For the poor in the early part of Victoria's reign work was a drudge and the hours long, and people had precious little free time to enjoy themselves. Most had no transport other than a cart or gig at their disposal, and had not travelled far beyond the boundaries of their own town or village. However, by the 1870s, the railways had threaded their way across the country, and Bank Holidays and half-day Saturdays had been made obligatory by Act of Parliament. All of a sudden the ordinary working man and his family were able to enjoy days out and see a little more of the world.

With characteristic business acumen, Francis Frith foresaw that these new tourists would enjoy having souvenirs to commemorate their days out. In 1860 he married Mary Ann Rosling and set out with the intention of photographing every city, town and village in Britain. For the next thirty years he travelled the country by train and by pony and trap, producing fine photographs of seaside resorts and beauty spots that were keenly bought by millions of Victorians. These prints were painstakingly pasted into family albums and pored over during the dark nights of winter, rekindling precious memories of summer excursions.

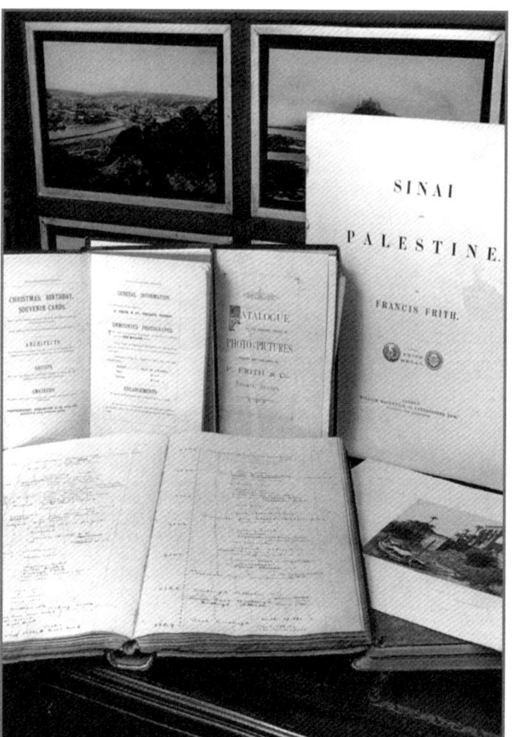


## The Rise of Frith & Co

Frith's studio was soon supplying retail shops all over the country. To meet the demand he gathered about him a small team of photographers, and published the work of independent artist-photographers of the calibre of Roger Fenton and Francis Bedford. In order to gain some understanding of the scale of Frith's business one only has to look at the catalogue issued by Frith & Co in 1886: it runs to some 670 pages, listing not only many thousands of views of the British Isles but also many photographs of most European countries, and China, Japan, the USA and Canada – note the sample page shown on page 9 from the hand-written *Frith & Co* ledgers detailing pictures taken. By 1890 Frith had created the greatest specialist photographic publishing company in the

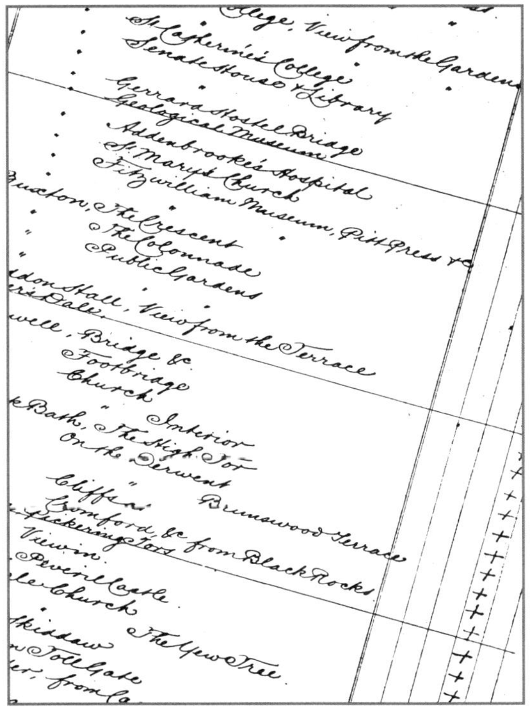
llege, View from the Gardens
St Catherine's College
Senate House & Library
Gerrard Hostel Bridge
Geological Museum
Addenbrooke's Hospital
St Mary's Church
Fitzwilliam Museum, Pitt Press &c
The Crescent
The Colonnade
Public Gardens
Hall, View from the Terrace
Bridge &c
Footbridge
Church
Interior
The High Tor
On the Derwent
Cliffs
Brunswood Terrace
Cromford, &c from Black Rocks
View in
Peveril Castle
Church
The Yew Tree
Toll Gate

world, with over 2,000 outlets – more than the combined number that Boots and WH Smith have today! The picture on the right shows the *Frith & Co* display board at Ingleton in the Yorkshire Dales (left of window). Beautifully constructed with a mahogany frame and gilt inserts, it could display up to a dozen local scenes.

### Postcard Bonanza

The ever-popular holiday postcard we know today took many years to develop. In 1870 the Post Office issued the first plain cards, with a pre-printed stamp on one face. In 1894 they allowed other publishers' cards to be sent through the mail with an attached adhesive halfpenny stamp. Demand grew rapidly, and in 1895 a new size of postcard was permitted called the court card, but there was little room for illustration. In 1899, a year after Frith's death, a new card measuring 5.5 x 3.5 inches became the standard format, but it was not until 1902 that the divided back came into being, with address and message on one face and a full-size illustration on the other. *Frith & Co* were in the vanguard of postcard development, and Frith's sons Eustace and Cyril continued their father's monumental task, expanding the number of views offered to the public and recording more and more places in Britain, as the coasts and countryside were opened up to mass travel.

Francis Frith died in 1898 at his villa in Cannes, his great project still growing. The archive he created continued in business for another seventy years. By 1970 it contained over a third of a million pictures of 7,000 cities, towns and villages. The massive photographic record Frith has left to us stands as a living monument to a special and very remarkable man.

# Frith's Archive: *A Unique Legacy*

**Francis Frith's** legacy to us today is of immense significance and value, for the magnificent archive of evocative photographs he created provides a unique record of change in 7,000 cities, towns and villages throughout Britain over a century and more. Frith and his fellow studio photographers revisited locations many times down the years to update their views, compiling for us an enthralling and colourful pageant of British life and character.

We tend to think of Frith's sepia views of Britain as nostalgic, for most of us use them to conjure up memories of places in our own lives with which we have family associations. It often makes us forget that to Francis Frith they were records of daily life as it was actually being lived in the cities, towns and villages of his day. The Victorian age was one of great and often bewildering change for ordinary people, and though the pictures evoke an impression of slower times, life was as busy and hectic as it is today.

**See Frith at www.francisfrith.co.uk**

We are fortunate that Frith was a photographer of the people, dedicated to recording the minutiae of everyday life. For it is this sheer wealth of visual data, the painstaking chronicle of changes in dress, transport, street layouts, buildings, housing, engineering and landscape that captivates us so much today. His remarkable images offer us a powerful link with the past and with the lives of our ancestors.

## Today's Technology

Computers have now made it possible for Frith's many thousands of images to be accessed almost instantly. In the Frith archive today, each photograph is carefully 'digitised' then stored on a CD Rom. Frith archivists can locate a single photograph amongst thousands within seconds. Views can be catalogued and sorted under a variety of categories of place and content to the immediate benefit of researchers.

Inexpensive reference prints can be created for them at the touch of a mouse button, and a wide range of books and other printed materials assembled and published for a wider, more general readership. The day-to-day workings of the archive are very different from how they were in Francis Frith's time: imagine the herculean task of sorting through eleven tons of glass negatives as Frith had to do to locate a particular sequence of pictures! Yet the archive still prides itself on maintaining the same high standards of excellence laid down by

Francis Frith, including the painstaking cataloguing and indexing of every view.

It is curious to reflect on how the internet now allows researchers in America and elsewhere greater instant access to the archive than Frith himself ever enjoyed. Many thousands of individual views can be called up on screen within seconds on one of the Frith internet sites, enabling people living continents away to revisit the streets of their ancestral home town, or view places in Britain where they have enjoyed holidays. Many overseas researchers welcome the chance to view special theme selections, such as transport, sports, costume and ancient monuments.

We are certain that Francis Frith would have heartily approved of these modern developments in imaging techniques, for he himself was always working at the very limits of Victorian photographic technology.

## The Value of the Archive Today

Because of the benefits brought by the computer, Frith's images are increasingly studied by social historians, by researchers into genealogy and ancestory, by architects, town planners, and by teachers and schoolchildren involved in local history projects.

In addition, the archive offers every one of us an opportunity to examine the places where we and our families have lived and worked down the years. Highly successful in Frith's own era, the archive is now, a century and more on, entering a new phase of popularity.

## The Past in Tune with the Future

Historians consider the Francis Frith Collection to be of prime national importance. It is the only archive of its kind remaining in private ownership and has been valued at a million pounds. However, this figure is now rapidly increasing as digital technology enables more and more people around the world to enjoy its benefits.

Francis Frith's archive is now housed in an historic timber barn in the beautiful village of Teffont in Wiltshire. Its founder would not recognize the archive office as it is today. In place of the many thousands of dusty boxes containing glass plate negatives and an all-pervading odour of photographic chemicals, there are now ranks of computer screens. He would be amazed to watch his images travelling round the world at unimaginable speeds through network and internet lines.

The archive's future is both bright and exciting. Francis Frith, with his unshakeable belief in making photographs available to the greatest number of people, would undoubtedly approve of what is being done today with his lifetime's work. His photographs, depicting our shared past, are now bringing pleasure and enlightenment to millions around the world a century and more after his death.

# Essex - *An Introduction*

IN THE FILM *Four Weddings and a Funeral*, the funeral takes place in Essex.

This sounds like the answer to a question in a general-knowledge quiz, but there is a serious point to be made here: St Clement's church at West Thurrock is no more funereal than any other church in the country, but the location-manager of *Four Weddings* had nevertheless done well to find such a bizarre place. Quite simply, it has to be seen to be believed. Better still, one has to go there. Even the big screen does not adequately convey the way that the church is so utterly dwarfed by the huge industrial works looming behind it. They seem to fill the sky. Partly, it is a question of scale, and partly a question of juxtaposition. And, whilst the word 'juxtaposition' should not be used lightly, it is a word that is particularly applicable to Essex.

'County of contrasts': the phrase has probably been over-used by writers attempting to describe Essex, but like a lot of clichés, it is often the best phrase to use. That sense of contrast comes in many forms - old and new, big and small, attractive

and ugly, busy and remote - and, in the same way that a comedian needs a 'straight man', it is the friction between the two that gives Essex its magic.

Even so, different generations have seen different things in Essex. Early topographical writers concentrated on the county's fertility. The historian Thomas Fuller, writing in 1662, described it as 'a fair country plentifully affording all things necessary to man's subsistence'. More recently, it seems that many writers have been on the defensive when speaking of Essex. They stress that although it is not a landscape of extremes, the terrain is agreeable enough; they point out that whilst it has no impressively pinnacled cities, it possesses a number of sturdy manufacturing towns, and so on.

Being human, we like to categorise. Whilst we are keen to celebrate Essex's variety, we also want to think that it has a personality all of its own. Some counties, after all, seem to be a pick-and-mix of the counties that surround them - and it cannot be denied that Essex shares features with Kent, London, Hertfordshire, Cambridgeshire and Suffolk in the areas where it touches them. On the other hand, Essex does have a strong geographical identity. Apart from its north-west corner, its boundaries are defined by rivers or the sea; and elsewhere, Epping Forest draws a shaky line between Essex and what is now Greater London. The county could almost be one enormous stronghold.

At one point, that is virtually what it was: today's Essex is the descendant of the kingdom of the East Saxons. This was a notoriously undocumented enclave of Dark Age England, whose royal family were part-pagan, part-Christian characters who all insisted on names beginning with the letter S. We know little more than that, in fact. Whereas the other Saxon dynasties claimed direct descent from the god Woden, the kings of Essex linked themselves to a different deity, Saxnot. Perhaps even in this small quirk we can see Essex's desire to be different.

There was probably some neo-Arthurian whimsy at work when Essex County Council adopted the three seaxes - peculiarly-shaped Saxon daggers - for its coat of arms. Appearing on everything from civic buildings to cricket club ties, they form a tiny link to the county's distant past. Saxon Essex ceased to exist long before the Norman Conquest - but even then, it had had a long history.

Colchester - still marketed as 'Britain's oldest recorded town' - had been a tribal capital before the Romans arrived. The Romans made it an administrative centre of their own, and the town is still scattered with Roman remains, despite Boudicca's attempts to raze the place to the ground. With its two ends defined by Colchester and London, Essex was soon supplied with long, straight roads.

The Saxons themselves, though less given to civil engineering projects, left quite a legacy. They left their names in the names of their villages - Stybba, Tilli, Clacc; they left churches and earthworks. Look at a map of Witham, for instance, and see how the circular ramparts of the Saxon hill-fort fossilised themselves into the shapes of streets.

Essex reached its boom-time in the Middle Ages. It is important to remember that the boom was created by ordinary people, working hard with whatever natural resources the landscape could lay at their door. The centre of Essex, for instance, is a great mass of London clay. It has always made good wheat-growing country. Towns like Braintree, Chelmsford, Colchester and Saffron Walden all had their stately Corn Exchanges, self-confident neo-Classical affairs with pillars and pediments. No less influenced by the landscape was the woollen industry. Essex's numerous fast-flowing rivers were ideal for operating the mills necessary for the wool trade. Coggeshall and Dedham were among the places to benefit.

Much later, when wool ceased to be important, a godsend came in the manufacture of imitation silk: Courtaulds established silk-works at Bocking and Halstead, for example, and immediately became major employers. Populations that had previously subsisted on cottage industries like straw-plaiting soon found themselves ensconced in the new mills. Other places had their own livelihoods: Earls Colne had its ironworks, Thaxted its maltings.

Prosperity is always apt to shape itself into buildings, and Essex, with no native stone, had to be imaginative in its choice of materials. That is partly why so little remains of the great forest that once enveloped the county. Epping Forest, Hatfield Forest, Hockley Woods and Writtle Forest only represent a fraction of what was once here. One only has to see the number of half-timbered houses illustrated in this book to appreciate wood's importance here as a building material. Even a number of church towers were made of wood. When the timber thinned out, there were other resources at hand: Essex began to churn out bricks, and to use them with gay abandon. It is inspiring to think that Layer Marney Towers, for example, began as a pile of bricks (31548, page 76).

As grand as its history may have been, Essex should not be viewed in complete isolation. Nowhere in Britain has grown-up in a void. All of the Home Counties, in particular, have a love-hate relationship with London. The capital's proximity can be beneficial in terms of trade and transport, but the Home Counties also risk becoming London's back yard. Essex was perhaps especially unfortunate in this respect: the East End became equated early on with London's less well-to-do housing and its grimier industries, and these soon crept over the border. Before the 1965 boundary changes, it seemed that a vast chunk of the East End was neither London nor Essex. Consider, too, how Essex contains one of London's seaside-resorts (Southend), two of its New Towns (Harlow and Basildon), and its third airport (Foulness and Willingale had been considered, too, before the decision was made to expand Stansted). Virtually every town in the county is now fair game for London commuters. But then, if London was further away, several of Essex's towns and villages would probably not exist. Look at Brentwood: it started life as a humble chapelry of South Weald that just happened to occupy a prime position on a main road. Roads meant coaching; coaching meant trade; and trade meant a town.

Of course, this is just one face of Essex. We only have to travel as far north as Braintree before the

accents become more East Anglian than Estuarine. Much of the county is still largely agricultural. Along the rivers and the shoreline, there are still miles of sparsely-inhabited wilderness. Lots of Essex people can tell tales about getting lost on the marshes. It is possible, too, to be a few hundred yards from the edge of an Essex town, and yet ostensibly be in the middle of the countryside.

This is not the Essex of the public consciousness. It is always foolhardy to generalise about a region or country, but it is often the most garish and colourful aspects of a place that grab the outsider's imagination. Since the 1980s, of course, Essex natives have had to listen to oft-repeated witticisms about 'Essex man' and 'Essex girls'. Preconceptions are difficult things to overturn. Take the hills, for example. Steep gradients are not something that many people would connect with Essex. Yet the north of the county is decidedly rolling, and a brisk walk up Halstead High Street or Maldon's Market Hill has been known to change the mind of many a disbeliever.

So Essex can be seen as a county where the normal seems abnormal; where ordinariness rubs shoulders with surprises. This book takes us to a failed spa, a Pierrot show, and a water-tower named after an elephant. It incorporates turn-of-the-century markets and 1950s beaches. We will visit buildings that have been swept away by bombs, storms, and changes of fashion, and buildings that stand as firm today as they did 100 years ago.

Our tour, as it happens, starts at Purfleet - only a stone's throw from that churchyard where the mourners laid Simon Callow's character to rest, the wind tousled Hugh Grant's hair, and the rain fell. Of course, films and photographs are not the real thing, but they can make good introductions. The truth, as they say, is out there; and the pictures in this book are a useful cross-section of something that is proud, unique, and ultimately three-dimensional. Essex awaits.

**Chelmsford, High Street 1892** 31508

# Purfleet to Maldon

**Purfleet**
**The Royal Hotel c1950** P148001

This hotel was built in 1828 on the site of an earlier pub called The Ship. It went through a number of names before a visit from Edward VII ensured that it became The Royal. It was, indeed, famous for the 'assemblage of beauty and fashion' that flocked here for its evening concerts, its cuisine, and its Botanic Gardens.

**Aveley, High Street c1952** A110014
Aveley is a large Thames-side village that grew up in the shadow of the great mansion, Belhus. The house was a significant employer in Aveley. Much added-to in recent years, the High Street retains a core of old buildings, including The Crown & Anchor (left). The pub's name reflects the village's nautical inclinations.

**South Ockendon, The Windmill c1960** S280022
South Ockendon's smock mill - seen here across the moat of a long-vanished hall - was built c1829. It may have stood on the site of an ancient watermill. By the 1960s, it was apparently 'dirty grey with gaping holes torn in the sides'. Much-buffeted by the winds, it finally collapsed altogether in 1977.

▼ **Grays, The Square c1945** G85016
The Magistrates' Court (centre left) was built in 1930 as a police station. An earlier police station had stood in the same position. The war memorial, on the other hand, occupies the site of a horse-trough and a urinal.

▼ **Socketts Heath, The Parade, Lodge Lane c1955** S277002
This part of Grays was developed in the 1930s. This road, Lodge Lane, was then the main A13, linking Southend and London. In the foreground is Albert Winn's confectioner's, with its well-stacked window display. Other shops include Grays Co-op and Stanley Barker's butcher's. The girls' white shoes and socks are typical of the mid 50s.

▲ **Bulphan, The Old Plough House c1955** B323001
Appleton's Farm was built in the 15th century. One of the Appletons, Sir Henry, engaged the Dutch engineers who worked on the Thames seawalls 300 years ago. During the 20th century, the farm became the Old Plough House Refreshment Rooms. It is still a well-known restaurant in this low-lying fenland area.

◄ **Stanford le Hope, The View Looking North c1960** S258028

This is the High Street, seen from the tower of St Margaret's Church. Like neighbouring Corringham, Stanford was enlarged in the 1920s and 30s to accommodate workers from the nearby oil refineries. The grand-looking building with the triangular pediment is the Methodist church.

▼ **Corringham, Church Road c1955** C243022
Corringham still has some old buildings. The Bull dates largely from the 17th century, though the wing on the right, with its projecting gable, is two centuries older. Like so many pubs round here, it has smuggling associations; it is riddled with sliding panels, double doors and secret chambers. A weekly animal market used to be held outside.

▼ **Hadleigh, The Castle 1891** 29070
The Castle had long been a romantic ruin, over-run with ivy and brushwood, when Constable painted it. At the time of this photograph it was already 'much resorted to in summer by picnic parties', said a guide-book. The four corner towers - of which only two survive to any great height - have walls nine feet thick at the base.

▲ **Canvey Island, Shell Beach c1955** C237005
A good study of a 1950s beach. There are no shadows, and most of the holidaymakers are well wrapped up. The chap in the braces (left) does not look particularly warm. Nevertheless, the Riverside Café is there in the distance to provide sustenance. The structure on the left is still used today as a snack-bar and lifeguard-station.

**Rayleigh, High Road c1955** R224009

Rayleigh has come a long way from the 'wild she-goat clearing' suggested by its name. Here we see one of the town's post-offices. Beyond the row with the Co-op hoarding ('More than a thousand service-points in London & Southend') are the Sunday School (1902) and the Wesleyan church (1885).

**Southend-on-Sea, The Statue of Queen Victoria 1898** 41388

Southend was always proud of its royal credentials. Various royals, including Queen Victoria's fourth daughter, Princess Louise, had stayed here at different times. This statue was erected by Bernard Tolhurst, the town's ex-mayor, the year before the photograph was taken. It originally stood on Pier Hill, but is now on the cliff-top.

**Southend-on-Sea, The Beach c1950** S155004

With a scattering of bare torsos and heavily-tanned forearms, this view is sunnier than many Essex beach-scenes. The apparatus in the centre is a windlass for hauling boats up onto the beach. It is obviously a shingly beach, too, judging by the slightly pained-looking walk of the people emerging from the sea.

◄ **Southend-on-Sea, The 'Golden Hind' c1960** S155079
Southend is not where one might expect to find Drake's famous ship. In fact, this is a full-sized replica, built in 1949 by twelve local mariners. Madame Tussaud's provided wax figures of Sir Francis and his crew. In recent years, it has been replaced by another facsimile ship: Blackbeard's *Queen Anne's Revenge*.

► **Hockley, The Spa Hotel c1960** H176035
A spa was established at Hockley after 1838, when a Mrs Clay claimed that she had been cured of asthma by a well in her garden. A pump-room and a hotel were built in 1843, but spas were already becoming outmoded. The hotel gradually gained a low reputation, and it was where the village poor came to collect their dole.

◄ **Paglesham, The River Roach c1955** P143012
Paglesham once relied on three things: agriculture, boat-building and oysters. In the 1870s there were up to 100 boats and 200 people engaged in the oyster-fishery here. The 20th century, however, saw the oysters blighted by disease, floods and harsh winters, and the industry finally petered out in the 1970s. Pleasure-craft rule here now.

**Hullbridge, The River Crouch c1960** H179084
Hullbridge gained popularity in the 1930s as a mini-resort. It was one of the few places on the Crouch with direct access to the water, hence the attraction for bathers. Its jetties also proved useful for the transportation of building materials. Here we see a number of large rowing-boats that have been converted into house-boats.

**Hullbridge, from South Woodham Ferrers c1960** H179028
Although the Woodham-Hullbridge ferry was discontinued in 1948, the Crouch is still fordable at this point. It is a venture that should not be taken lightly, however. There is known to have been a bridge here in the 16th century - but a story that it was later blown up by Parliamentarian soldiers is nothing more than fantasy.

**Althorne, The Corner c1955** A107006
Althorne is a long village above the River Crouch. Connected to London by rail, it manages to combine a commuting population with a number of working farms. The Dutch-style weatherboarded cottages next to the Black Lion pub provide an interesting contrast with some of the newer developments.

**Burnham-on-Crouch, High Street c1955** B325012
This is evidently a hot day in Burnham. Sashes and casements have been flung open; both the convertibles have their hoods down, and one of them has stopped at the tea-shop. In the foreground, the Ford is travelling with its windscreen cranked open (an option on some models).

**Tillingham, St Nicholas's Church c1955** T115001
Tillingham has been owned by the Dean and Chapter of St Paul's since at least 604. They were responsible for building several of the weatherboarded cottages on the green - or the Square, as it is called. This space was used to host peddlers' fairs and sporting events, all under the watchful eye of the 14th-century church-tower.

WALLWORTH

**Maldon, High Street 1891** 29078

This part of the High Street suffered a disaster soon after this picture was taken. A fire broke out in Ortewell's ironmongers (beyond the white gable, right) in January 1892. The conflagration destroyed several shops, including Fullers, though Archer's 'millinery & mantles' on the corner survived. The brick wall encloses the former St Peter's Church - now a library.

THE LONDON CENTRAL MEAT Co LTD
POOLE
BEEF!
PRINTING
RICHARD POOLE
PICTURE POSTCARDS

**Maldon, High Street 1906** 55544
The Moot Hall, in the middle of the picture, was built c1435 by a member of the D'Arcy family. Initially a defensible tower, it was later given over to civic purposes: a court and a police station were housed here. Until 1974 the council used to meet in the room above the clock. The Hall was much shaken by the 1884 earthquake.

**Heybridge, St Andrew's Church 1901** 46720
This church, with its seemingly unfinished tower, is an important example of 12th-century architecture. The round-headed doorways and windows are typically Norman. The south door is notable, too, for its iron scrollwork. One of Heybridge's main industries, an ironworks, surrounded the church and vicarage on three sides.

◄ **Maldon, The Promenade 1909** 62098

Maldon was once full of flourmills, maltings, ropewalks and boatyards. It was a significant port, too, handling corn, coal, chalk and hay. The boat in the foreground looks distinctly like a pleasure-craft, though, to judge by that slatted seat. The church is St Mary's, which doubled as a seamark for the mariners.

▼ **Maldon, Beeleigh Abbey 1895** 35662

Beeleigh was a house of Premonstratensians. It was founded in 1180 (replacing an earlier house at Parndon), though it became a private residence after the Dissolution. It was at this time, too, that the timbered and brick-nogged wing on the right was put up. The site was rather dilapidated until a major restoration in 1912.

◄ **Langford, The Village 1895** 35665

St Giles's Church is virtually unique in possessing an apse at its west end - apses (rounded ends) usually occur at the east of churches. This is a Norman church, rebuilt in the 1880s. Langford was entirely agricultural until the arrival of a water-pumping and treatment plant in the 1920s. It employed around 50 local men.

**Little Baddow, Grace's Walk 1906** 56895
This point - where Grace's Walk crosses Sandon Brook - has a ghost-story attached to it: Lady Alice Mildmay (d1615), child-bride of Sir Henry, supposedly drowned herself in a pond here after he was unkind to her. It is likely that the tale was invented - or at least embellished - by Jesse Berridge, who was rector of Little Baddow from 1915 to 1947. He used it as the basis for a novel called *Gracy's Walk*.

**Little Baddow, The Rodney 1903** 50240
The Rodney is a pub with a tangled history. In fact, it has been two pubs with the same name. The one in the photo is the 'Old' Rodney, which in turn gave its name to the adjacent sixteen acres of brake and heather. A pleasure garden was established here in 1885 by one Elijah Mecklenberg.

**Woodham Walter, The Bell 1903** 50245
The Bell (left) was 'well-situated for trade in the populous and respectable village of Woodham Walter', said one advertisement. The tradition that it was built the same year as the church (1563) seems improbable. In its heyday, The Bell had a tap-room, two parlours, three bedrooms, three attics, beer- and liquor-cellars, a bake-office and a brew-office.

**Danbury, The Palace 1906** 56899
Danbury Palace was built in the 1830s to the designs of Susan Constantia Round. She was afraid of fires, and so gave the house three staircases - three potential fire-escapes. Constructed on the site of the Mildmay family's 16th-century mansion, this extravagant mock-Tudor palace was the home of the Bishops of Rochester between 1845 and 1892.

**Springfield, The Plough 1906** 56901
This was the main London-Colchester road. Stage-coaches used to change horses at The Plough (right). The pub is the one feature of this scene to stay relatively unchanged. The smithy, opposite, has given way to a garage; and the row of cottages (with a sign saying 'Cyclist's Rest') are long-since demolished.

**East Hanningfield, Willis Farm c1960** E255012
There are three Hanningfields - East, West and South. Their name means 'open country of Hana's people'. Willis Farm is a timber-framed and plastered structure just outside The Tye, as the centre of East Hanningfield is known. The chimney-stacks and jutting gables indicate the house's 16th-century origins.

BARCLAY AND COMPANY LIMITED
R S P C A
APRIL

# Chelmsford to Great Waltham

**Chelmsford, Tindal Square 1906** 56881
To the forefront stands a horse-trough supplied by the RSPCA. Over to the right is one of the enterprises that would have kept the horses busy - Walter Catt's grocery, with its cart parked outside. The Chelmsford Window Cleaner was more self-sufficient: his handcart is just visible behind the Coal & Coke Merchants' shop.

**Chelmsford, The Shire Hall 1895** 35515
Note the man with the roller (centre), flattening the pathway: a necessary job in the days of dirt roads. Frederick Spalding's shop (photography and picture-framing, right) seems to be attracting a degree of interest. Next door is Henry Cleale's ironmongery, with enamel bowls outside; and in the foreground is James Wray's draper's.

**Chelmsford, The Marconi Works 1919** 69028
It is midday. The Marconi works had sprung up in 1912 opposite the goods yard and cattle pens belonging to the railway. Guglielmo Marconi had first established his firm in Chelmsford in 1899. In actual fact, much of the workforce pictured here is probably coming from Hoffman's, the famous ball-bearing works further up the street.

**Widford, The White Horse 1906** 56908
Widford has two pubs: the Sir Evelyn Wood (named after the great Victorian military hero) and this one. There was also once a Silent Woman - its non-PC inn-sign depicted a lady with no head. The cottages were pulled down in the 1930s, when the new A12 cut a swathe through the village.

**Writtle, The Green c1955** W154017
This corner of Writtle has not altered: the pump and the cottages are still there. The house to the right was originally a maltings - the structure with the lantern was the oast-house. It belonged to the Writtle Brewery Company until they were taken over by Truman's. It also contained timbers from the demolished Lordship Hunting Lodge.

◄ **Ingatestone, High Street 1925** 78742
Ingatestone's livelihood came from its position on the London-Chelmsford road. Even the 'stone' in its name may refer to a milestone. The Spread Eagle (left) - its frontage reading 'Commercial & Posting House' - offered garage and stabling facilities through its archway. The pub also hosted cricket lunches and other social functions.

◄ **Blackmore, The Bull c1955**
B320002
Blackmore has always been a village of contrasts: this scene includes a modern double-decker bus and a Ford Popular. It also combines 20th-century housing with the late 15th-century Bull. The lane at the pub's right-hand side is called Little Jordan - a punning reference to Blackmore's most famous building, Jericho Priory.

▼ **Ingatestone, The Hall The Gateway c1955** I10012
Ingatestone Hall was built in 1548 by Sir William Petre. The gateway was remodelled and given its turret in the 18th century: it boasts a one-handed clock and the Petres' motto ('Without God, Nothing'). The family were recusant Catholics, and there are two priest-holes concealed in the house. Queen Elizabeth came to stay here in 1561.

◄ **Billericay The Chantry Café c1955** B319013
A chantry was established in Billericay in 1342. The Chantry Café probably occupies the site of the priest's house. The building - with the date 1510 on its gable - is reputedly where four local Puritans met before sailing to the New World aboard the Mayflower. There is a Billerica (no 'y') in Massachusetts to this day.

▼ **Billericay, Chapel Street c1960** B319069
The substantial building behind the trees is Billericay church, which was rebuilt in 1780, though retaining its fine 15th-century brick tower. Goodspeeds ('Best Buy: Fine Fat English Plaice 2/2 a lb') was originally part of The Chequers Inn, the bulk of which lies just outside our picture, to the left. The half-timbered house dates from c1450.

▼ **East Horndon, Herongate Village 1907** 57587
Herongate, in the parish of East Horndon, supposedly takes its name from a gate crossing the road near The Boar's Head. The manor house, Heron Hall, was the home of the Tyrell family, many of whom are commemorated in East Horndon church. It was one of their ancestors who is traditionally implicated in the 'accidental' death of William Rufus.

▲ **East Horndon The Boar's Head Pond, Herongate 1908** 60602
The pub and pond are named after the crest of the Tyrell family: a boar's head with a peacock-feather in its jaws. The inn has spurious Dick Turpin connections, involving leaps from upper windows. Slightly more definite is that Ralph Vaughan Williams passed this way when collecting folk-songs. He may well have called in at The Boar's Head.

**Great Warley**
**The Thatcher's Arms 1906**

53506

Oak Beam Cottage, Two Door Cottage, and Chestnut Tree Cottage lead us to The Thatcher's Arms (left). Its sign reads: 'Says the Thatcher to his man, Tom what dost thou think/Can we raise the ladder? Yes Master first let us drink./Says Tom to his Master, the Ladder's raised high./I must have some ale I'm always a-dry'. Well, quite.

**South Weald Queen Mary's Chapel 1906** 54457

This 16th-century lodge, set in what was the walled kitchen-garden of Weald Hall, has unsubstantiated associations with (pre-Bloody) Queen Mary. The story is that she stayed here and observed Mass in the 1540s, whilst still a Princess. Weald Hall itself was demolished in 1950.

**Brentwood High Street 1895**

35668

Although it did not achieve parish status until 1873, Brentwood's position on the main road ensured it was always commercially busy. Here we see David Rist's grocery, with the piled tins in the window (right), and next door, Percy Crowe's furniture store. Crowe also owned three drapers' shops and a tailor's in Brentwood.

**Brentwood, Queen's Road 1896** 38653
The corner-shop is Henry Gutteridge the baker's. According to the stencilled advertisement above the boy's head, they specialised in 'Birthday & Christmas Cakes'. The area to the left with two tall trees was known as the Shrubbery. It was the garden of Colonel Fielder, who owned Fielder's Brewery in King's Road (to the left). There is a roundabout here now.

**Brentwood, The Asylum 1897** 39874
The County Lunatic Asylum was opened in 1853, though it was being constantly enlarged. 'The wards are airy, many commanding an extensive prospect', said Kelly's Directory. The grounds comprised 'a farm, kitchen-gardens & pleasure grounds; the farm and garden being cultivated by patients under the superintendence of attendants'. Visiting was limited to once a fortnight.

**Shenfield, The Place 1906** 54464
Shenfield - meaning 'fair open country' - is now an eastward extension of Brentwood. The Place was designed by Robert Hooke in 1689. It was formerly home to the Courage family. Inside, many of the rooms have their original panelling and cornices, and there is an elaborate staircase with twisted balusters.

**Kelvedon Hatch, The Common, The Stocks 1906** 54476
Kelvedon Hatch is a popular commuter village in the Green Belt north-west of Brentwood. It is now well-known for its formerly 'secret' government nuclear bunker. The village's focus is its pond, and the two pubs that flank it. The stocks can be found at the junction of Blackmore Road and Stocks Lane.

◄ **Ongar, High Street c1955**

O19003

A castle was built here after the Conquest. A 'chipping' (market) soon grew up outside the gates. This view shows the King's Head, which bears the date 1697. Ongar was an important staging-post for carriers, passenger-coaches and wagons. In 1717, the town's first postmaster was earning a yearly salary of £25.

**Ongar, The Grammar School 1923** 74825
One Richard Stokes founded Ongar Academy in 1811 for 'twenty young gentlemen'. It later became the Grammar School. By the turn of the century, it was able to boast a 'Grand tepid swimming bath ... Pure milk from own dairy farm. Diet unlimited. Cricket, tennis, fishing. Terms 30 guineas inclusive; reduction for brothers'.

**Ongar, The Lodge, Shelley c1950** 019023
Shelley is a parish north of Ongar, consisting of a Victorian church, a hall, and a handful of houses and farms. The Hall was built in the 15th century. Despite a restoration in 1869, it still retains some fine Elizabethan oak carvings. This picture shows its lodge on the main Ongar-Dunmow road.

**Fyfield, Queen Street c1955** F80007
Once known as Fyfield Street, or just The Street, this end of the village now takes its name from The Queen's Head pub. The building level with the pushchair (just visible in the middle of the road) is the old schoolhouse. The school - founded by Dr Anthony Walker in 1687 - has since relocated to new premises.

**Abridge, Market Place c1960** A106017
Abridge was always well-supplied with pubs and tea-rooms. Here we see The Blue Boar with its fine Tuscan porch (left), and opposite, The Retreat (now the post office). The low building next to The Boar was once Whitbread's Beer Stores, from which cartloads of beer used to be delivered daily to London.

**Chigwell Row, Manor Road c1960** C240004
Chigwell Row was laid-out along the edge of Hainault Forest in the 18th century. By the 1840s it boasted 'many mansions and good residences, occupied by London businessmen and others'. Just to the right of our picture, there were once some tea-gardens and a temperance retreat. 'Genteel company' also flocked to the Chigwell Row Races each August.

**Chigwell, The King's Head Hotel 1906** 55245
The King's Head was immortalised as The Maypole in *Barnaby Rudge*. Dickens described it as having 'more gable ends than a lazy man would care to count on a sunny day'. He borrowed the name from a Maypole inn at nearby Chigwell Row. 'Chigwell, my dear fellow, is the greatest place in the world', he wrote to a friend.

**Chigwell, The Grammar School 1925** 78726

The school was founded in 1629 by Samuel Harsnett, Archbishop of York. He had once been vicar of Chigwell. The school's original core, on the left, now houses the library. The headmaster's house (right) was a later addition. By 1899, facilities included an open-air swimming-bath, a sanatorium, and an Officers' Training Corps armoury.

**Loughton, High Road c1955** L106006

Loughton's population boomed after the railway arrived in 1850. This shot includes Overy's hairdresser's, the post office, Charlton's newsagent's, and (on the extreme left) the Century Cinema. The latter was opened in 1928 by the actress Evelyn Laye. Although much-loved, it was demolished in 1965 and replaced by shops.

**Epping, Cottages at Upshire c1955** E38028
Upshire is a small settlement at the north-west corner of Epping Forest. This row of attractive weatherboarded cottages stands close to its Victorian church. Local tradition (prompted by the writings of Suetonius) places Boudicca's final defeat and suicide at Upshire.

TRUST
HOUSE
THE GREEN DRAGON.
WALTHAM ABBEY POST OFFICE
E.J.RIPLEY

**Waltham Abbey, Market Square 1921**

70158

This picture is a marvellous slice of social history. Look at the goods for sale: cheeses, zinc bathtubs, wicker baskets. One can only speculate as to the purpose of the anatomical diagram in the centre foreground: is the stallholder a quack? It looks as though he is about to make a sale. Notice how absolutely everybody wears a hat.

▼ **Nazeing, The Red Lion c1955** N66005
Nazeing's name means 'settlers on the projection of land'. It sits above the River Lea, and is a world of arable fields and market-garden glasshouses. The Red Lion, in the hamlet of Middle Street, was rebuilt in 1888; it is now a residence called the White House. The car outside is a pre-war Morris.

▼ **Roydon, Nether Hall c1955** R229004
Nether Hall was the home of the Colt family. This great 15th-century mansion was demolished in 1773 - all except this gatehouse, which proved just too sturdy. The Colts' fortune came from Sir Thomas, Privy Councillor to Edward IV. His brass is in the church. It was one of his daughters, Jane, who married Sir Thomas More.

▲ **Harlow, Mulberry Green c1955** H22014
The Green Man, at Mulberry Green, may well be Harlow's oldest pub. It dates from the 16th century. Once a coaching-inn, it lost out when the London-Newmarket road was re-routed in the 1850s. A carnival used to be held here in the 1920s and 30s, as well as a notoriously rowdy Whit Monday fair. Note the smithy on the left.

◄ **Roydon, The War Memorial c1955** R229008
Roydon was once a market-town. A fair that used to be held every August (to mark St Peter's Day) lapsed during the Great War. The small dark shed on the left is in fact a 19th-century lock-up. Next to it - immediately behind one of the white posts - are the village stocks.

◄ **Sheering, The Crown Inn c1960** S274005
Despite its proximity to Harlow and the M11, Sheering still retains the appearance of a village and a sense of community. Parked here, outside the Crown, is that epitome of 1960s social history, the Mk I Cortina. These majestic vehicles are much prized by classic car enthusiasts the world over.

◀ **Harlow, Welfords Corner c1955** H22026

Harlow was a clothing town that had gone into something of a decline. It had once had a market and, until the 19th century, a celebrated cattle fair. The project of Harlow New Town was initiated in 1947, to draw off some of London's surplus population. Old Harlow, seen here, still manages to retain a separate identity.

▼ **Hatfield Heath, The Clipped Hedge Tea-Rooms c1955** H172002

In medieval times, Clipped Hedge was supposedly the only building situated on Hatfield Heath itself. The Heath was an area of common land criss-crossed by roads. It became an ecclesiastical parish in 1860. These tea-rooms were established between the wars by Margaret Goddard to take advantage of the passing trade.

◀ **Hatfield Broad Oak, Market Square c1965** H171007

The place-name allegedly refers to 'a tree of extraordinary bigness' that once stood in Hatfield Forest. The tree is now called the Doodle Oak. The Market Square is notable for the Cock's elaborate ironwork bracket, and for the famously wonky timbered carriageway (centre right).

**High Easter, The Cock & Bell c1960** H175010
The Cock & Bell was granted its licence in 1615, following a petition from the villagers. The house beside it, with the overhang, was once a shop; it may have been one in Tudor times. The grey building in the centre of the picture is a former butcher's shop called the Cock & Rother shop ('rother' meaning cattle).

**Great Waltham, Chelmsford Road c1965** G101005
The Mini van heralds the swinging 60s. Next to the post office, Snow's the butchers were well-known for their Piggy Porker sausages - indeed, they used to advertise them on the side of their delivery-van. This delicacy probably went down well with Vitbe (left). Snow's is now a house called, appropriately, No 1 Snows Court.

**Little Leighs, Leez Priory, The Inner Gatehouse 1903** 50582
Leez Priory was a house of Austin Canons, founded in the 12th century. After the Dissolution it fell to Lord Rich, who built a new mansion on the site in 1536. Little remains of his house, except two gatehouses, and traces of gardens and fishponds. There is also a conduit-head (right), made from reused stone from the monastery.

HORN HOTEL
THE HORN
COMMERCIAL
HOTEL
ANNUAL SHOW
£60

# Braintree to Colchester

**Braintree, High Street 1900** 46241
The building with the clock and columns (left) was Braintree's Corn Exchange. Built in 1839, it survived until the 1960s. The clock was spared, and can still be seen in its old position. The Horn was a 17th-century coaching inn with a cobbled courtyard. It provided nourishment for the farmers driving hard bargains two doors away.

▼ **Braintree, Rayne Road 1900** 46243
The Methodist church on Sandpit Road corner was demolished in July 1988 to make way for the George Yard shopping precinct. It had opened in 1868. The tall house in the distance is Twyford House; John Bunyan once stayed in an earlier building on the site. During the First World War, it was a hostel for female munitions workers.

▼ **Braintree, High Street 1902** 48277
Cook's the butchers (right) were 'noted for sausages and pork pies', according to their fascia. The shop on the extreme right later made way for the Central Cinema, although it has long since reverted to shopping purposes. Down the street, just to the right of the white canopy, was the entrance to West's brush factory - one of Braintree's key industries.

▲ **Braintree, Bank Street 1903** 50561
Bank Street underwent an unexpected transformation in February 1941, when this corner was destroyed by a bomb. Only three years earlier, the 15th-century half-timbered 'island' in the middle of the street had been removed in a road-widening measure. Here, it is Frederick Pluck's - supplier of boots, shoes, woollens and tailoring.

**Bocking, Cane's Mill 1900** 46251
Built in 1580 by the Nottage family, this was originally a fulling mill, though it was being used for corn by the 19th century. The wooden road bridge had to be replaced in 1926: it was rotting, and traffic was becoming heavier. There is a classical-style bridge of steel and stone there now, decorated with Bocking's armorial bearings.

**Bocking, Church Street 1902** 48287
Bocking's row of almshouses was endowed by the MP John Doreward in 1440. Standing close to the River Pant, they have often suffered flooding - the most recent occasion being in October 2001. The Workmen's Hall, in the foreground, was built in 1899 by the Courtauld family as a place of recreation for the employees at their mill.

▲ **Bocking, The Convent 1900** 46252
The Convent Chapel was constructed in 1899 by Sir John Francis, who was also responsible for Westminster Cathedral. It served as the main Catholic church for Braintree & Bocking until 1939. Fulling Mill House, to the right, was once home to the Nottages, who built Cane's Mill. Later, the artist and philanthropist Edith Arendrup lived there.

► **Rayne, All Saints' Church 1901** 46726
Rayne's original church was Norman. Prayers offered there were considered particularly beneficial to pregnant women. This striking brick tower was built c1510 for Sir William Capel. It is a masterly combination of blue-brick decoration, angular turrets and castellated friezes. The remainder of the church was fully rebuilt in 1840.

**Black Notley, The Watermill 1903** 50579
Black Notley's 17th-century mill was fed by a tributary of the River Brain. It was later used as a garage, but was demolished just prior to the Second World War. Its pond was filled in, and this scene has now been radically changed by road-widening and housing. The pub down the road, The Vine, continues to hold its own.

**Cressing, The Street 1909** 62125
Cressing is an expanding village just to the south of Braintree. It has its own railway-station, formerly known as Bulford station. The house on our left, with the lofty fir trees, is called The Firs to this day. The cottage opposite was at one time the village post office.

▼ **White Notley, The Street 1903** 50577
The Cross Keys (left) dates from the 17th century, though it replaced an earlier structure. Until the 19th century, there was a brewery here too. Just beyond it stood the village lock-up (built 1828). In the 1990s, Black and White Notley were joined by a new, purpose-built sibling, Great Notley.

▼ **Witham, St Nicholas' Church 1900** 46229
The original hub of Witham was here, at Chipping Hill. As the town grew, its businesses drifted off to the main London-Colchester road. St Nicholas' was built c1330. The cottages were pulled down in 1935: the workmen apparently received a bonus for clearing the rubble in time for an important wedding.

▲ **Witham, Newland Street 1900** 46227
The Constitutional Club (far left) burned down in February 1910. The blaze also damaged Archer's ironmongers' shop next door (with a kettle for its trade-sign). Spectators at the fire faced the added danger of having the clock fall on them. Notice the contrast, here, between the children's fashions and those of the slightly older girl.

**Kelvedon, Gray's Mill 1925** 78738

There has been a mill here since Saxon times - and perhaps earlier, as Kelvedon is believed to be the site of the Roman station Canonium. This particular mill, built in 1850 following a fire, was driven by water and steam. It ceased working shortly before the Great War, and has recently been converted into five flats.

**Layer Marney The Towers 1892** 31548
This magnificent eight-storey gatehouse was built by Sir Henry, 1st Lord Marney, in the 1520s. The rest of the mansion he had planned was never built: Sir Henry died in 1523, and the Marneys were extinct two years later. The Towers, however, are admired for their sheer scale, and for the terracotta ornamentation on their parapets.

◄ **Tiptree, Messing Maypole Mill c1955** T116021

Tiptree Heath was 'a miserable barren piece of land' haunted by tinkers, squatters, and horse-racing fans. In 1775 a brick tower-mill was built near the crossroads by John Matchett, a Colchester millwright. Though no longer working in the 1950s, it still looked smart with its black cap, finial ball and lightning conductor. It is now a house.

▼ **Tollesbury, High Street c1955** T117010

Tollesbury is a large maritime village whose green has long since become a grassless square. Its church, behind the photographer, is famous for its inscribed font urging the congregation not to swear. Pewter's, second from the right, sold sweets and haberdashery.

◄ **Wivenhoe The Waterfront c1960** W160043

In the middle-distance are Wivenhoe's oyster-sheds: they were built on stilts so that the tide could feed the oysters in their beds underneath. The site is now occupied by Wivenhoe Sailing Club. The pointed roof on the other bank belongs to St Laurence's Church, Rowhedge, built in 1838 as a pastiche of York Minster's chapter-house.

◄ **Great Bentley, The Green and the Pond 1892** 31542
There were once several ponds on the green: this is now the only one. The house on the left - The Laurels - is now, indeed, called Pond House. In 1943 the green was ploughed in a 'dig for victory' experiment to grow potatoes, flax and peas; but the soil proved too poor, and the scheme was abandoned.

**Great Bentley, The Green 1892** 31541
At 42 acres, Great Bentley's village green is the largest in England. In its time, it has held tea-parties, dancing, football, cricket, flower shows, horse-races and prize-fights. The Hardingham family were well-placed to see all these things from their workshop (right). They were wheelwrights, undertakers and blacksmiths, all rolled into one.

**St Osyth, The Ship c1910** S38301
St Osyth (generally pronounced 'Toosey') recognised the benefits of tourism early on, as witnessed by the rack of picture-postcards for sale on the left. The woman in front of The Ship is wearing rather dated clothes for 1910 - the outfits of the women in the background are more representative of the period.

**St Osyth, The Creek 1912** 64261
St Osyth once had thriving lime-kilns and maltings, as well as wharves and a tide-mill. There was already a corn-mill here in 1413. Its successor, pictured here, was built c1730, but was damaged by the weather and by a mine during the Second World War. It finally collapsed in the 1960s.

**Jaywick, 'B' Type Bungalow c1955** J4027

The farmland that became Jaywick was originally sold off after the agricultural depression of the late 1920s. Chalets - intended as holiday-homes only - were built on the available plots. The district council, indeed, felt that the area was unsuited to permanent development. By the 1950s, however, Jaywick was an established resort.

**Clacton-on-Sea, Christchurch 1891** 28234

Clacton's Christchurch was only four years old at the time of this photograph. Closer to us stands the lifeboat house, built in 1878 with an endowment from the Freemasons. The fencing had been added 'to protect it from damage from cattle'. In 1934 it was acquired by Fitch Motors, engineers and bus-operators. Later it became a pub.

**Clacton-on-Sea, The Passmore Edwards Holiday Home 1901** 46693
John Passmore Edwards (d1911) was a newspaper magnate and philanthropist. He contributed half the cost of erecting this holiday-home for deprived children. It opened in 1899; this home had been preceded by a building in Carnarvon Road. The venture was part of a scheme by the Sunday School Union.

**Clacton-on-Sea, Station Road 1904** 51537
This is a good cross-section of late-Victorian fashions: the ladies' headgear varies from straw boaters to elaborate bonnets. The bicycle with the oil-bath also has a string guard to protect the rider's skirt. Occupying the corner, right of centre, is Thorogood's ('Fancy Pastry Cook') - originally built as the town's first post office in the early 1870s.

PIER PAVILION
GRAND CONCERTS
Lessee_HAROLD MONTAGUE.
BATHING
FROM STEAMBOAT LANDING
TICKETS AT PIER ENTRANCE
HOT & COLD SEA WATER.
ICES TEAS

**Clacton-on-Sea**
**The Pier with a Belle Steamer 1907** 58937
The pier had something for everyone: for a shilling, one could have a session of 'Character Reading: Head, Face & Hand'. Other distractions were provided by the Pavilion and the camera obscura. Alternatively, one could hop on one of the fleet of Belle Steamers that plied daily to a number of other coastal destinations.

◄ **Great Holland, The Ship Inn c1955** G274014
The Ship was once famous for its quoits lawn. It hosted the annual Peachey Quoits Cup Championship - Mr Peachey was the owner of some nurseries in the village. One wonders if the quoits were made at the local foundry, Ratcliff's, whose usual output was shears and other agricultural implements.

◄ **Clacton-on-Sea, The Beach and the Yorkshire Pierrots 1912** 64237A

Pierrot shows arrived in England in 1891. Fred Pullan's Yorkshire troupe opened in Clacton in 1901. An early handbill described them as 'Up to Date - Thoroughly Refined'. The show came to an end when a gale destroyed the stage in August 1912. By this time, in any case, Pierrots were being supplanted by non-costumed 'fol-de-rol' entertainers.

▼ **Frinton-on-Sea The Greensward 1921** 70292

Frinton's development as a resort began as late as 1885, by which time Walton and Clacton were both well-established. Frinton grew at a slower, more genteel pace. Instead of sea-front amusements, it has the long stretch of cliff-top pastureland known as the Greensward, and the imposing 1896 pile of the Grand Hotel.

◄ **Walton-on-the-Naze, The Promenade 1891** 28238

Walton-le-Soken was an agricultural and beachcombing parish that expanded into Walton-on-the-Naze in the 1820s. Its early visitors were upper-class people who had summer homes here. Even the Pre-Raphaelites came. The arrival of the railway in 1867, and the 1872 National Bank Holiday Act, opened Walton up to everybody.

**Walton-on-the-Naze, High Street 1921** 70289
The High Street was laid out when Walton became a tourist destination, and it soon had shops to cater for most needs. On the right, for example, is Share's cycle-shop, also diversifying into 'furniture, lino etc'. Such old buildings as Walton ever possessed had been engulfed by the sea. The church dates only from 1873.

**Dovercourt, High Street c1955** D51006
The pinnacle belongs to the Dovercourt & Harwich Co-operative Society. Built in 1902, it housed their store, as well as a billiards room, a reading room, and a concert hall. Nearer to the camera is the gas showroom (with its 'Mr Therm' logo on the fascia), and level with the four-legged litter-bin is Doris Fryatt's sweet-shop.

**Harwich, The High Lighthouse c1955** H150008
A nine-sided tower of white brick, the High Lighthouse is Harwich's most striking feature. It was constructed in 1818 by John Rennie Senior, a civil engineer, although there had been a lighthouse on this spot since 1664. However, shifting sands meant that the course of the channel changed, and the lighthouse was redundant by 1863.

◄ **Colchester, The Asylum 1891** 28217
Colchester Asylum was erected in 1840 as a hotel serving the nearby railway station. However, it was not successful, and took on a different role in 1859. It boasted 'everything necessary for the purposes of a training school and home for persons of a feeble mind, including gymnastic apparatus and workshops'. It was demolished in 1986.

◄ **Dedham, High Street and Church 1907** 57548
Described in the 1880s as a 'small, quaint, and decayed town', Dedham's prosperity had climaxed in the early 1500s. It was essentially a wool town, and its great market was held in the wide stretch of road we see here. The house with the classical pediment is Sherman's, formerly a school teaching English and maths.

▼ **Colchester, The Castle 1891**
28215
Colchester had the largest castle-keep ever built in Europe. Constructed in 1080, its floor plan is half as big again as the White Tower's. It stands above a temple dedicated to Claudius's victory of AD43. Though reduced from three storeys to two in the 1680s, the castle is still imposing. It now houses a museum of Roman artefacts.

◄ **Colchester, North Hill and the Market 1892**
31522
Looking up towards St Peter's Church, it is easy to appreciate Colchester's early appeal as a defensive settlement: the steep approaches would always have stood in its favour. Here on the right is the town's cattle-market. Formerly in the High Street, it moved to this more capacious site in 1862.

**Colchester, The Water-Tower 1907** 57541
Known as Jumbo, this 105ft tower was built in 1882 - the same year that the famous elephant had arrived at London Zoo. Nikolaus Pevsner observes that it is 'no doubt meant to be Roman in spirit', in keeping with the town's sense of its own antiquity. In 2001, there were plans afoot to convert it into a block of flats.

**Colchester, Scheregate 1921** 70363
Scheregate, the lane in the centre, sits astride Colchester's town wall. The house straddling Scheregate Steps replaces a Roman postern. The 16th-century premises of H F Smith are now a shop dealing in ethnic ornaments, whilst the barber's shop (see the stripy pole) now sells antiques. The girl's panama hat is typical of the period.

**Lexden, St Leonard's Church 1892** 31545
When it was rebuilt in 1821, several observers found St Leonard's 'by no means handsome'. The rather apologetic little chancel was replaced by a grander model two years after this picture was taken. Lexden is dotted with Roman earthworks, and it has been suggested that the church may stand on the site of a temple.

# Coggeshall to Clavering

**Coggeshall, Church Street c1955** C242015
Coggeshall was an agricultural town that turned to cloth-making in the Middle Ages. Many of its houses date from this period. The timber-framed Cockrells is 16th-century, though it is pre-dated by the white building next door: in our photo, this is 'Arthur Hutley - Removal & Haulage Contractor'. Hutley also ran a bus company.

**Coggeshall, The Woolpack Inn c1955** C242006
Though a 15th-century building, The Woolpack seems only to have been an inn since 1708. Before that, it was the home of Coggeshall's Puritan vicar Thomas Lowrey, who had been ejected from the living in 1660. Thereafter, he ministered to independent congregations from this house. The inn was once called The Woolpack & Punchbowl.

**Earls Colne, High Street 1961** E67027
Earls Colne is a large industrial village on the A604: silk-winding, brick-making, seed-growing, and iron-founding have all taken place here. The Lion is a 16th-century building that may have once been a market house - facing, as it does, onto the market place. Note the proliferation of television aerials in this scene.

**Halstead, Trinity Street c1955** H168001
We are standing with our backs to the level crossing - although Halstead was soon to lose its railway. The balustraded Colne Valley Cinema, right (later the Savoy), was built in 1907 on the site of The Railway Bell pub. It is now a Chinese takeaway. The Public Gardens, behind the Guinness poster (left), were opened in 1901.

**Sible Hedingham, The View from the Churchyard c1960** S276012
Sible Hedingham is a large village in the Colne Valley. It was once well-known for its hops, and for its toy-works. St Peter's Church contains a cenotaph to Sir John Hawkwood, a Hedingham tanner's son who became a highly-respected mercenary in 14th-century Florence. Uccello painted an equestrian portrait of him.

▼ **Castle Hedingham, Pye Corner c1965** C238007
Hedingham's dominant feature, the enormous castle keep, looms behind these cottages just to the right, out of picture. Bones were recently unearthed in a garden at Pye Corner. It has been suggested that they belonged to soldiers who fell in battles of the early 1200s. It is all a far cry from the smart sports saloon and the Mini.

▼ **Great Yeldham, The Oak c1960** G324026
Yeldham Oak - seen here in the background - is now a hollow stump held together with cement and iron bands. These accoutrements were provided by public subscription in 1949, when the oak was already reputed to be a thousand years old. A new tree had been planted next to it in 1863, to commemorate the Prince of Wales's wedding.

▲ **Finchingfield, The Green c1965** F77075
This must be the best-known view in Essex. Where would manufacturers of calendars be without it? The squat church-tower, the steadily clambering roofs, and the central pond all combine to make a satisfying, unsophisticated scene. In the foreground is the Old Poor House: note its original 16th-century chimneys and casements.

**Great Bardfield, Brook Street 1903** 50565

Great Bardfield once had market rights, but it is now a quiet village. The fountain in Brook Street (left) was installed in 1861 by Henry Smith of Bardfield Hall. It pumped water from a spring in Hall Meadows. The Smiths were great benefactors: they also presented Bardfield with its own fire-engine.

**Wethersfield**
**The Green 1903**
50571
The house with the criss-crossing is The Red Lion (right). One 19th-century landlord was also the village blacksmith, and the pub served as a hospital in the Great War. In 1806 the young Patrick Brontë came to Wethersfield as a curate. What classics would his brood have produced had they grown up here rather than at Haworth?

**Great Saling St James' Church 1903**
50564
This is the manorial core of Saling: the church and the hall. St James' dates from the 12th century, but its early details have been obscured by Victorianisation. The Hall is a 17th-century extravaganza in blue and red brick, with curvilinear gables. It contains some fine oak panelling.

◄ **Shalford, Braintree Road 1909** 62121
The cottages on the right were almshouses. They are gone now. The white house just past them is known as the Penthouse - a name connected with the fact that the village pound (or 'pent') for stray cattle once stood here. In the street, the nanny is pushing a pram of an unusual penny-farthing design.

▼ **Stebbing, High Street c1965** S282002
Stebbing ('the village of Stybba's people') stretches for a mile between its two ends - Bran End and Church End. The High Street, running parallel to Stebbing Brook, boasts a castle mound and a wealth of old houses. Church Farm, beyond the war memorial, is 16th-century.

◄ **Dunmow, The Town Hall c1960** D90069
Dunmow's Market Place is otherwise known as Rood End. The Town Hall, in its original form, was built in 1578. Dunmow ceased to be a borough in 1885, and the building has since housed various commercial enterprises. The Saracen's Head, across the road, allegedly once had a part-time highwayman for a landlord.

**Dunmow, High Street c1955** D90010
The White House (behind the cenotaph, right) is now the offices of Uttlesford District Council. It was once a convent. Dunmow used to be a busy thoroughfare town: The White Lion, farthest from the camera, was a coaching inn. Here, the pre-war van and the stationary Hillman give little indication of any congestion.

**Great Easton, The Endway c1960** G95008
Great Easton stands on a rise above the River Chelmer, which is here little more than a stream. The church of St John and St Giles is a largely 12th-century structure with a much-maligned wooden bell-tower. Just behind the churchyard lie the remains of a castle: a 20ft motte surrounded by a dry ditch.

**Thaxted, The Post Office 1906** 55463
In the Middle Ages, Thaxted was one of the most prosperous towns in Essex. Its wealth came from its cutlers and, later, its maltings. 'But', said a Victorian guide-book, 'these industries have now deserted it; its market is lost; its houses are decaying; and its population is rapidly declining'. Now, it is something of a tourist-trap.

**Thaxted, The Almshouses 1906** 55464
Thaxted's mill was built in 1804 by John Webb, a local landowner whose brick and tile-works provided the building materials. The almshouses sprang from certain medieval endowments that were re-channelled into charity purposes. The row on the left (called the Chantry) was originally built as a priest's house.

◄ **Stansted Mountfitchet, Stansted Hall c1965**

S281034

These days, Stansted is best known for its airport. Half a mile away stands the Hall - a neo-Jacobean brick mansion, built in 1871 on the site of an earlier structure. It has extensive grounds, including a lake called the Black Pond. In the late 20th century, the Hall became the Arthur Findlay College for the Advancement of Physical Science.

◄ **Elsenham, Fullers End c1960** E231001

Fuller's End (named after a 13th-century Walter Fullo) was the site of Elsenham's first railway station. The line is just out of sight, where the road bends behind the house. The steep gradient on this part of the line - a precipitous 1 in 107 - made the station unworkable, and in 1847 it was moved to its present site.

▼ **Stansted Mountfitchet, Chapel Hill c1965** S281010

Herrington's window (right) is a treasure-trove of 1960s grocery products: Lyons Swiss Rolls, Brooke Bond Tea, Woodbines, and Bev. It later became the NatWest Bank. The two pubs featured here are The King's Arms (far left) and, up the hill, The Barley Mow. The latter is now a house.

◄ **Stansted Mountfitchet, Lower Street c1965** S281013

Earlier in the century, the half-timbered building housed a pair of shops. They are now private dwellings. Like the white house next door, they date from the 16th century. The parish pump used to stand on the corner of Grove Hill, just in front of Stansted Park Stores (the polygonal building on the right).

**Newport, Belmont Hill 1932** 85126
We are looking out of the village, towards the former toll bridge over Wicken Water. The timber-framed house dates from the late 15th or early 16th century, though it was extended later on. The woman's short-skirted summer dress and cloche hat are typical of the early 1930s.

▼ **Newport, Crown House 1932** 85127
Crown House started life as The King's Head. It was a late 16th-century building that underwent a makeover in 1692: this was when the shell-hood was added to the doorway, the pargework (or decorative plasterwork) executed, and the pub's name changed to The Crown. There is no substance to the myth that Nell Gwynn ever lived here.

▼ **Saffron Walden, Market Place 1907** 58809
By the middle of the 19th century, the farms around Saffron Walden had largely converted from sheep to grain. The Corn Exchange (right) replaced the old Woolstaplers' Hall in 1849. It escaped demolition itself after trading ceased, and in 1975 became a library and arts centre. The building with the mock-Tudor frontage is the Town Hall.

▲ **Saffron Walden Bridge Street 1907**
58810
The houses on the left were built in the late 15th century, before oak grew scarcer. Hence the heavy, narrow-spaced timber-framing. The Eight Bells, on the right, was built as a private house in the 16th century. Its carved bressumers are original. The inn's name moved here from Hill Street in the 1840s.

◄ **Saffron Walden Fry's Gardens 1907** 58821
Fry's Gardens, otherwise Bridge End Gardens, were initiated by Francis Gibson, a member of a well-known Quaker family. The grounds included a rose garden, vegetable and fruit gardens, and a maze of yew hedges. The latter (pictured here) was not open to the public, but the key could be obtained from Mr Swan (in the bowler hat).

**Saffron Walden, Hart's Yard 1919** 69138

This is the entrance to Hart's print works. Established in 1836, the firm was run by three generations of Harts, and still exists. Halfway down the yard on the left is The Tailor's Arms, which was destroyed by fire in 1930. One of the posters advertises a visit by the evangelist Gipsy Smith.

**Saffron Walden, King Street 1937** 88021
The Hoops is a 16th-century building that probably originated as a merchant's house with shops on the ground floor. It is now a smart restaurant. Of similar vintage was The Rose & Crown - the white building facing us in the distance. It burned down on Boxing Day 1969. Eleven people died.

**Audley End, The Mansion c1910** A109044
Audley End, just outside Saffron Walden, was built in 1603-16 for Thomas Howard, 1st Earl of Suffolk. He ruined himself by spending public funds on the house - hardly surprising, since the bill came to £190,000. It cost £500 alone to obtain the preliminary designs from Italy.

**Littlebury, The Village 1919** 69146
Littlebury's name, 'little fort', refers to pre-Roman earthworks in the parish. The village sits on the Roman road to Chesterford and Cambridge. This was the home of Henry Winstanley (b1644), architect of the first Eddystone lighthouse. He died when the building itself was destroyed by a storm.

**Clavering, Church End 1959** C241001
Clavering had one of the few pre-Conquest castles in England. Its later prosperity, deriving from corn and wool, helped to build the magnificent church. The long building with the overhang was the 15th-century guild-hall, serving Clavering's two guilds. It later became almshouses, and is now a cottage.

# Index

# Frith Book Co Titles

## www.francisfrith.co.uk

The Frith Book Company publishes over 100 new titles each year. A selection of those currently available is listed below. For latest catalogue please contact Frith Book Co.
***Town Books*** 96 pages, approximately 100 photos. ***County and Themed Books*** 128 pages, approximately 150 photos (unless specified). All titles hardback with laminated case and jacket, except those indicated pb (paperback)

| Title | ISBN | Price |
|---|---|---|
| Amersham, Chesham & Rickmansworth (pb) | 1-85937-340-2 | £9.99 |
| Andover (pb) | 1-85937-292-9 | £9.99 |
| Aylesbury (pb) | 1-85937-227-9 | £9.99 |
| Barnstaple (pb) | 1-85937-300-3 | £9.99 |
| Basildon Living Memories (pb) | 1-85937-515-4 | £9.99 |
| Bath (pb) | 1-85937-419-0 | £9.99 |
| Bedford (pb) | 1-85937-205-8 | £9.99 |
| Bedfordshire Living Memories | 1-85937-513-8 | £14.99 |
| Belfast (pb) | 1-85937-303-8 | £9.99 |
| Berkshire (pb) | 1-85937-191-4 | £9.99 |
| Berkshire Churches | 1-85937-170-1 | £17.99 |
| Berkshire Living Memories | 1-85937-332-1 | £14.99 |
| Black Country | 1-85937-497-2 | £12.99 |
| Blackpool (pb) | 1-85937-393-3 | £9.99 |
| Bognor Regis (pb) | 1-85937-431-x | £9.99 |
| Bournemouth (pb) | 1-85937-545-6 | £9.99 |
| Bradford (pb) | 1-85937-204-x | £9.99 |
| Bridgend (pb) | 1-85937-386-0 | £7.99 |
| Bridgwater (pb) | 1-85937-305-4 | £9.99 |
| Bridport (pb) | 1-85937-327-5 | £9.99 |
| Brighton (pb) | 1-85937-192-2 | £8.99 |
| Bristol (pb) | 1-85937-264-3 | £9.99 |
| British Life A Century Ago (pb) | 1-85937-213-9 | £9.99 |
| Buckinghamshire (pb) | 1-85937-200-7 | £9.99 |
| Camberley (pb) | 1-85937-222-8 | £9.99 |
| Cambridge (pb) | 1-85937-422-0 | £9.99 |
| Cambridgeshire (pb) | 1-85937-420-4 | £9.99 |
| Cambridgeshire Villages | 1-85937-523-5 | £14.99 |
| Canals And Waterways (pb) | 1-85937-291-0 | £9.99 |
| Canterbury Cathedral (pb) | 1-85937-179-5 | £9.99 |
| Cardiff (pb) | 1-85937-093-4 | £9.99 |
| Carmarthenshire (pb) | 1-85937-604-5 | £9.99 |
| Chelmsford (pb) | 1-85937-310-0 | £9.99 |
| Cheltenham (pb) | 1-85937-095-0 | £9.99 |
| Cheshire (pb) | 1-85937-271-6 | £9.99 |
| Chester (pb) | 1-85937-382 8 | £9.99 |
| Chesterfield (pb) | 1-85937-378-x | £9.99 |
| Chichester (pb) | 1-85937-228-7 | £9.99 |
| Churches of East Cornwall (pb) | 1-85937-249-x | £9.99 |
| Churches of Hampshire (pb) | 1-85937-207-4 | £9.99 |
| Cinque Ports & Two Ancient Towns | 1-85937-492-1 | £14.99 |
| Colchester (pb) | 1-85937-188-4 | £8.99 |
| Cornwall (pb) | 1-85937-229-5 | £9.99 |
| Cornwall Living Memories | 1-85937-248-1 | £14.99 |
| Cotswolds (pb) | 1-85937-230-9 | £9.99 |
| Cotswolds Living Memories | 1-85937-255-4 | £14.99 |
| County Durham (pb) | 1-85937-398-4 | £9.99 |
| Croydon Living Memories (pb) | 1-85937-162-0 | £9.99 |
| Cumbria (pb) | 1-85937-621-5 | £9.99 |
| Derby (pb) | 1-85937-367-4 | £9.99 |
| Derbyshire (pb) | 1-85937-196-5 | £9.99 |
| Derbyshire Living Memories | 1-85937-330-5 | £14.99 |
| Devon (pb) | 1-85937-297-x | £9.99 |
| Devon Churches (pb) | 1-85937-250-3 | £9.99 |
| Dorchester (pb) | 1-85937-307-0 | £9.99 |
| Dorset (pb) | 1-85937-269-4 | £9.99 |
| Dorset Coast (pb) | 1-85937-299-6 | £9.99 |
| Dorset Living Memories (pb) | 1-85937-584-7 | £9.99 |
| Down the Severn (pb) | 1-85937-560-x | £9.99 |
| Down The Thames (pb) | 1-85937-278-3 | £9.99 |
| Down the Trent | 1-85937-311-9 | £14.99 |
| East Anglia (pb) | 1-85937-265-1 | £9.99 |
| East Grinstead (pb) | 1-85937-138-8 | £9.99 |
| East London | 1-85937-080-2 | £14.99 |
| East Sussex (pb) | 1-85937-606-1 | £9.99 |
| Eastbourne (pb) | 1-85937-399-2 | £9.99 |
| Edinburgh (pb) | 1-85937-193-0 | £8.99 |
| England In The 1880s | 1-85937-331-3 | £17.99 |
| Essex - Second Selection | 1-85937-456-5 | £14.99 |
| Essex (pb) | 1-85937-270-8 | £9.99 |
| Essex Coast | 1-85937-342-9 | £14.99 |
| Essex Living Memories | 1-85937-490-5 | £14.99 |
| Exeter | 1-85937-539-1 | £9.99 |
| Exmoor (pb) | 1-85937-608-8 | £9.99 |
| Falmouth (pb) | 1-85937-594-4 | £9.99 |
| Folkestone (pb) | 1-85937-124-8 | £9.99 |
| Frome (pb) | 1-85937-317-8 | £9.99 |
| Glamorgan | 1-85937-488-3 | £14.99 |
| Glasgow (pb) | 1-85937-190-6 | £9.99 |
| Glastonbury (pb) | 1-85937-338-0 | £7.99 |
| Gloucester (pb) | 1-85937-232-5 | £9.99 |
| Gloucestershire (pb) | 1-85937-561-8 | £9.99 |
| Great Yarmouth (pb) | 1-85937-426-3 | £9.99 |
| Greater Manchester (pb) | 1-85937-266-x | £9.99 |
| Guildford (pb) | 1-85937-410-7 | £9.99 |
| Hampshire (pb) | 1-85937-279-1 | £9.99 |
| Harrogate (pb) | 1-85937-423-9 | £9.99 |
| Hastings and Bexhill (pb) | 1-85937-131-0 | £9.99 |
| Heart of Lancashire (pb) | 1-85937-197-3 | £9.99 |
| Helston (pb) | 1-85937-214-7 | £9.99 |
| Hereford (pb) | 1-85937-175-2 | £9.99 |
| Herefordshire (pb) | 1-85937-567-7 | £9.99 |
| Herefordshire Living Memories | 1-85937-514-6 | £14.99 |
| Hertfordshire (pb) | 1-85937-247-3 | £9.99 |
| Horsham (pb) | 1-85937-432-8 | £9.99 |
| Humberside (pb) | 1-85937-605-3 | £9.99 |
| Hythe, Romney Marsh, Ashford (pb) | 1-85937-256-2 | £9.99 |
| Ipswich (pb) | 1-85937-424-7 | £9.99 |
| Isle of Man (pb) | 1-85937-268-6 | £9.99 |
| Isle of Wight (pb) | 1-85937-429-8 | £9.99 |
| Isle of Wight Living Memories | 1-85937-304-6 | £14.99 |
| Kent (pb) | 1-85937-189-2 | £9.99 |
| Kent Living Memories(pb) | 1-85937-401-8 | £9.99 |
| Kings Lynn (pb) | 1-85937-334-8 | £9.99 |

**Available from your local bookshop or from the publisher**

# Frith Book Co Titles (continued)

| Title | ISBN | Price |
|---|---|---|
| Lake District (pb) | 1-85937-275-9 | £9.99 |
| Lancashire Living Memories | 1-85937-335-6 | £14.99 |
| Lancaster, Morecambe, Heysham (pb) | 1-85937-233-3 | £9.99 |
| Leeds (pb) | 1-85937-202-3 | £9.99 |
| Leicester (pb) | 1-85937-381-x | £9.99 |
| Leicestershire & Rutland Living Memories | 1-85937-500-6 | £12.99 |
| Leicestershire (pb) | 1-85937-185-x | £9.99 |
| Lighthouses | 1-85937-257-0 | £9.99 |
| Lincoln (pb) | 1-85937-380-1 | £9.99 |
| Lincolnshire (pb) | 1-85937-433-6 | £9.99 |
| Liverpool and Merseyside (pb) | 1-85937-234-1 | £9.99 |
| London (pb) | 1-85937-183-3 | £9.99 |
| London Living Memories | 1-85937-454-9 | £14.99 |
| Ludlow (pb) | 1-85937-176-0 | £9.99 |
| Luton (pb) | 1-85937-235-x | £9.99 |
| Maidenhead (pb) | 1-85937-339-9 | £9.99 |
| Maidstone (pb) | 1-85937-391-7 | £9.99 |
| Manchester (pb) | 1-85937-198-1 | £9.99 |
| Marlborough (pb) | 1-85937-336-4 | £9.99 |
| Middlesex | 1-85937-158-2 | £14.99 |
| Monmouthshire | 1-85937-532-4 | £14.99 |
| New Forest (pb) | 1-85937-390-9 | £9.99 |
| Newark (pb) | 1-85937-366-6 | £9.99 |
| Newport, Wales (pb) | 1-85937-258-9 | £9.99 |
| Newquay (pb) | 1-85937-421-2 | £9.99 |
| Norfolk (pb) | 1-85937-195-7 | £9.99 |
| Norfolk Broads | 1-85937-486-7 | £14.99 |
| Norfolk Living Memories (pb) | 1-85937-402-6 | £9.99 |
| North Buckinghamshire | 1-85937-626-6 | £14.99 |
| North Devon Living Memories | 1-85937-261-9 | £14.99 |
| North Hertfordshire | 1-85937-547-2 | £14.99 |
| North London (pb) | 1-85937-403-4 | £9.99 |
| North Somerset | 1-85937-302-x | £14.99 |
| North Wales (pb) | 1-85937-298-8 | £9.99 |
| North Yorkshire (pb) | 1-85937-236-8 | £9.99 |
| Northamptonshire Living Memories | 1-85937-529-4 | £14.99 |
| Northamptonshire | 1-85937-150-7 | £14.99 |
| Northumberland Tyne & Wear (pb) | 1-85937-281-3 | £9.99 |
| Northumberland | 1-85937-522-7 | £14.99 |
| Norwich (pb) | 1-85937-194-9 | £8.99 |
| Nottingham (pb) | 1-85937-324-0 | £9.99 |
| Nottinghamshire (pb) | 1-85937-187-6 | £9.99 |
| Oxford (pb) | 1-85937-411-5 | £9.99 |
| Oxfordshire (pb) | 1-85937-430-1 | £9.99 |
| Oxfordshire Living Memories | 1-85937-525-1 | £14.99 |
| Paignton (pb) | 1-85937-374-7 | £7.99 |
| Peak District (pb) | 1-85937-280-5 | £9.99 |
| Pembrokeshire | 1-85937-262-7 | £14.99 |
| Penzance (pb) | 1-85937-595-2 | £9.99 |
| Peterborough (pb) | 1-85937-219-8 | £9.99 |
| Picturesque Harbours | 1-85937-208-2 | £14.99 |
| Piers | 1-85937-237-6 | £17.99 |
| Plymouth (pb) | 1-85937-389-5 | £9.99 |
| Poole & Sandbanks (pb) | 1-85937-251-1 | £9.99 |
| Preston (pb) | 1-85937-212-0 | £9.99 |
| Reading (pb) | 1-85937-238-4 | £9.99 |
| Redhill to Reigate (pb) | 1-85937-596-0 | £9.99 |
| Ringwood (pb) | 1-85937-384-4 | £7.99 |
| Romford (pb) | 1-85937-319-4 | £9.99 |
| Royal Tunbridge Wells (pb) | 1-85937-504-9 | £9.99 |
| Salisbury (pb) | 1-85937-239-2 | £9.99 |
| Scarborough (pb) | 1-85937-379-8 | £9.99 |
| Sevenoaks and Tonbridge (pb) | 1-85937-392-5 | £9.99 |
| Sheffield & South Yorks (pb) | 1-85937-267-8 | £9.99 |
| Sherborne (pb) | 1-85937-301-1 | £9.99 |
| Shrewsbury (pb) | 1-85937-325-9 | £9.99 |
| Shropshire (pb) | 1-85937-326-7 | £9.99 |
| Shropshire Living Memories | 1-85937-643-6 | £14.99 |
| Somerset | 1-85937-153-1 | £14.99 |
| South Devon Coast | 1-85937-107-8 | £14.99 |
| South Devon Living Memories (pb) | 1-85937-609-6 | £9.99 |
| South East London (pb) | 1-85937-263-5 | £9.99 |
| South Somerset | 1-85937-318-6 | £14.99 |
| South Wales | 1-85937-519-7 | £14.99 |
| Southampton (pb) | 1-85937-427-1 | £9.99 |
| Southend (pb) | 1-85937-313-5 | £9.99 |
| Southport (pb) | 1-85937-425-5 | £9.99 |
| St Albans (pb) | 1-85937-341-0 | £9.99 |
| St Ives (pb) | 1-85937-415-8 | £9.99 |
| Stafford Living Memories (pb) | 1-85937-503-0 | £9.99 |
| Staffordshire (pb) | 1-85937-308-9 | £9.99 |
| Stourbridge (pb) | 1-85937-530-8 | £9.99 |
| Stratford upon Avon (pb) | 1-85937-388-7 | £9.99 |
| Suffolk (pb) | 1-85937-221-x | £9.99 |
| Suffolk Coast (pb) | 1-85937-610-x | £9.99 |
| Surrey (pb) | 1-85937-240-6 | £9.99 |
| Surrey Living Memories | 1-85937-328-3 | £14.99 |
| Sussex (pb) | 1-85937-184-1 | £9.99 |
| Sutton (pb) | 1-85937-337-2 | £9.99 |
| Swansea (pb) | 1-85937-167-1 | £9.99 |
| Taunton (pb) | 1-85937-314-3 | £9.99 |
| Tees Valley & Cleveland (pb) | 1-85937-623-1 | £9.99 |
| Teignmouth (pb) | 1-85937-370-4 | £7.99 |
| Thanet (pb) | 1-85937-116-7 | £9.99 |
| Tiverton (pb) | 1-85937-178-7 | £9.99 |
| Torbay (pb) | 1-85937-597-9 | £9.99 |
| Truro (pb) | 1-85937-598-7 | £9.99 |
| Victorian & Edwardian Dorset | 1-85937-254-6 | £14.99 |
| Victorian & Edwardian Kent (pb) | 1-85937-624-X | £9.99 |
| Victorian & Edwardian Maritime Album (pb) | 1-85937-622-3 | £9.99 |
| Victorian and Edwardian Sussex (pb) | 1-85937-625-8 | £9.99 |
| Villages of Devon (pb) | 1-85937-293-7 | £9.99 |
| Villages of Kent (pb) | 1-85937-294-5 | £9.99 |
| Villages of Sussex (pb) | 1-85937-295-3 | £9.99 |
| Warrington (pb) | 1-85937-507-3 | £9.99 |
| Warwick (pb) | 1-85937-518-9 | £9.99 |
| Warwickshire (pb) | 1-85937-203-1 | £9.99 |
| Welsh Castles (pb) | 1-85937-322-4 | £9.99 |
| West Midlands (pb) | 1-85937-289-9 | £9.99 |
| West Sussex (pb) | 1-85937-607-x | £9.99 |
| West Yorkshire (pb) | 1-85937-201-5 | £9.99 |
| Weston Super Mare (pb) | 1-85937-306-2 | £9.99 |
| Weymouth (pb) | 1-85937-209-0 | £9.99 |
| Wiltshire (pb) | 1-85937-277-5 | £9.99 |
| Wiltshire Churches (pb) | 1-85937-171-x | £9.99 |
| Wiltshire Living Memories (pb) | 1-85937-396-8 | £9.99 |
| Winchester (pb) | 1-85937-428-x | £9.99 |
| Windsor (pb) | 1-85937-333-x | £9.99 |
| Wokingham & Bracknell (pb) | 1-85937-329-1 | £9.99 |
| Woodbridge (pb) | 1-85937-498-0 | £9.99 |
| Worcester (pb) | 1-85937-165-5 | £9.99 |
| Worcestershire Living Memories | 1-85937-489-1 | £14.99 |
| Worcestershire | 1-85937-152-3 | £14.99 |
| York (pb) | 1-85937-199-x | £9.99 |
| Yorkshire (pb) | 1-85937-186-8 | £9.99 |
| Yorkshire Coastal Memories | 1-85937-506-5 | £14.99 |
| Yorkshire Dales | 1-85937-502-2 | £14.99 |
| Yorkshire Living Memories (pb) | 1-85937-397-6 | £9.99 |

**See Frith books on the internet at www.francisfrith.co.uk**

# Frith Products & Services

Francis Frith would doubtless be pleased to know that the pioneering publishing venture he started in 1860 still continues today. Over a hundred and forty years later, The Francis Frith Collection continues in the same innovative tradition and is now one of the foremost publishers of vintage photographs in the world. Some of the current activities include:

### *Interior Decoration*

Today Frith's photographs can be seen framed and as giant wall murals in thousands of pubs, restaurants, hotels, banks, retail stores and other public buildings throughout the country. In every case they enhance the unique local atmosphere of the places they depict and provide reminders of gentler days in an increasingly busy and frenetic world.

### *Product Promotions*

Frith products are used by many major companies to promote the sales of their own products or to reinforce their own history and heritage. Frith promotions have been used by Hovis bread, Courage beers, Scots Porage Oats, Colman's mustard, Cadbury's foods, Mellow Birds coffee, Dunhill pipe tobacco, Guinness, and Bulmer's Cider.

### *Genealogy and Family History*

As the interest in family history and roots grows world-wide, more and more people are turning to Frith's photographs of Great Britain for images of the towns, villages and streets where their ancestors lived; and, of course, photographs of the churches and chapels where their ancestors were christened, married and buried are an essential part of every genealogy tree and family album.

### *Frith Products*

All Frith photographs are available Framed or just as Mounted Prints and Posters (size 23 x 16 inches). These may be ordered from the address below. From time to time other products - Address Books, Calendars, Table Mats, etc - are available.

### *The Internet*

Already fifty thousand Frith photographs can be viewed and purchased on the internet through the Frith websites and a myriad of partner sites.

For more detailed information on Frith companies and products, look at these sites:

www.francisfrith.co.uk
www.francisfrith.com
*(for North American visitors)*

See the complete list of Frith Books at:

***www.francisfrith.co.uk***

This web site is regularly updated with the latest list of publications from the Frith Book Company. If you wish to buy books relating to another part of the country that your local bookshop does not stock, you may purchase on-line.

***For further information, trade, or author enquiries please contact us at the address below:***

**The Francis Frith Collection, Frith's Barn, Teffont, Salisbury, Wiltshire, England SP3 5QP.**
Tel: +44 (0)1722 716 376 Fax: +44 (0)1722 716 881 Email: sales@francisfrith.co.uk

**See Frith books on the internet at www.francisfrith.co.uk**

# FREE MOUNTED PRINT

**Mounted Print**
*Overall size 14 x 11 inches*

**Fill in and cut out this voucher and return** *it with your remittance for £2.25 (to cover postage and handling). Offer valid for delivery to UK addresses only.*

***Choose any photograph included in this book.*** *Your SEPIA print will be A4 in size. It will be mounted in a cream mount with a burgundy rule line (overall size 14 x 11 inches).*

**Order additional Mounted Prints at HALF PRICE (only £7.49 each*)**
If you would like to order more Frith prints from this book, possibly as gifts for friends and family, you can buy them at half price (with no additional postage and handling costs).

**Have your Mounted Prints framed**
For an extra £14.95 per print* you can have your mounted print(s) framed in an elegant polished wood and gilt moulding, overall size 16 x 13 inches (no additional postage and handling required).

*** IMPORTANT!**

**These special prices are only available if you order at the same time as you order your free mounted print. You must use the ORIGINAL VOUCHER on this page (no copies permitted). We can only despatch to one address.**

*Send completed Voucher form to:*
**The Francis Frith Collection, Frith's Barn, Teffont, Salisbury, Wiltshire SP3 5QP**

# CHOOSE ANY IMAGE FROM THIS BOOK

*Please do not photocopy this voucher. Only the original is valid, so please fill it in, cut it out and return it to us with your order.*

| Picture ref no | Page no | Qty | Mounted @ £7.49 | Framed + £14.95 | Total Cost |
|---|---|---|---|---|---|
| | | 1 | Free of charge* | £ | £ |
| | | | £7.49 | £ | £ |
| | | | £7.49 | £ | £ |
| | | | £7.49 | £ | £ |
| | | | £7.49 | £ | £ |
| | | | £7.49 | £ | £ |
| *Please allow 28 days for delivery* | | | * Post & handling (UK) | | £2.25 |
| | | | Total Order Cost | | £ |

Title of this book ...............................
I enclose a cheque/postal order for £ ...........
made payable to 'The Francis Frith Collection'

OR please debit my Mastercard / Visa / Switch / Amex card
*(credit cards please on all overseas orders),* details below

Card Number

Issue No (Switch only) Valid from (Amex/Switch)

Expires Signature

Name Mr/Mrs/Ms ..........................................
Address ..........................................
..........................................
..........................................
.......................... Postcode ..................
Daytime Tel No ..........................................
Email ..........................................

Valid to 31/12/05

Free Print - see overleaf

**Would you like to find out more about Francis Frith?**

We have recently recruited some entertaining speakers who are happy to visit local groups, clubs and societies to give an illustrated talk documenting Frith's travels and photographs. If you are a member of such a group and are interested in hosting a presentation, we would love to hear from you.

Our speakers bring with them a small selection of our local town and county books, together with sample prints. They are happy to take orders. A small proportion of the order value is donated to the group who have hosted the presentation. The talks are therefore an excellent way of fundraising for small groups and societies.

**Can you help us with information about any of the Frith photographs in this book?**

We are gradually compiling an historical record for each of the photographs in the Frith archive. It is always fascinating to find out the names of the people shown in the pictures, as well as insights into the shops, buildings and other features depicted.

If you recognize anyone in the photographs in this book, or if you have information not already included in the author's caption, do let us know. We would love to hear from you, and will try to publish it in future books or articles.

**Our production team**

Frith books are produced by a small dedicated team at offices in the converted Grade II listed 18th-century barn at Teffont near Salisbury, illustrated above. Most have worked with the Frith Collection for many years. All have in common one quality: they have a passion for the Frith Collection. The team is constantly expanding, but currently includes:

Jason Buck, John Buck, Ruth Butler, Heather Crisp, David Davies, Isobel Hall, Julian Hight, Peter Horne, James Kinnear, Karen Kinnear, Tina Leary, Stuart Login, Amanda Lowe, David Marsh, Sue Molloy, Kate Rotondetto, Dean Scource, Eliza Sackett, Terence Sackett, Sandra Sampson, Adrian Sanders, Sandra Sanger, Julia Skinner, Claire Tarrier, Lewis Taylor, Shelley Tolcher and Lorraine Tuck.